NAME THE AMERICAN MOVIE STAR ROMANTICALLY LINKED WITH ELVIS, WHO NEVER APPEARED IN ANY OF HIS FILMS?

WHAT WERE THE TITLES OF BOTH SIDES OF THE FIRST RECORD ELVIS CUT?

NAME THE TELEVISION SHOW ELVIS WAS TURNED DOWN FOR AFTER AUDITIONING?

IN WHAT MOVIE DID ELVIS PLAY A HELICOPTER CHARTER PILOT?

Here are some of the provocative queries about the man whose music became a worldwide phenomenon. If you know the answers to them, you're ready to prove yourself an Elvis expert with some of the oldies but goodies you'll find in—

THE ELVIS PRESLEY TRIVIA QUIZ BOOK

More Quiz Books from SIGNET

If you wish to order these titles,
please see the coupon in
the back of this book.

THE ELVIS PRESLEY TRIVIA QUIZ BOOK

by
Helen Rosenbaum

A SIGNET BOOK

NEW AMERICAN LIBRARY

TIMES MIRROR

*With special thanks to
Robert Earle Haynie, whose
guiding spirit behind this book
has been far from trivial.*

NAL BOOKS ARE ALSO AVAILABLE AT DISCOUNTS IN BULK
QUANTITY FOR INDUSTRIAL OR SALES-PROMOTIONAL USE.
FOR DETAILS, WRITE TO PREMIUM MARKETING DIVISION,
NEW AMERICAN LIBRARY, INC., 1301 AVENUE OF THE
AMERICAS, NEW YORK, NEW YORK 10019.

SIGNET TRADEMARK REG. U.S. PAT. OFF. AND FOREIGN COUNTRIES
REGISTERED TRADEMARK—MARCA REGISTRADA
HECHO EN CHICAGO, U.S.A.

SIGNET, SIGNET CLASSICS, MENTOR, PLUME AND MERIDIAN BOOKS
are published by The New American Library, Inc.,
1301 Avenue of the Americas, New York, New York 10019

FIRST SIGNET PRINTING, MAY, 1978

1 2 3 4 5 6 7 8 9

PRINTED IN THE UNITED STATES OF AMERICA

QUESTIONS

1. FACTS OF LIFE — AND BEYOND

1. Give the correct spelling of Elvis's middle name as it appears on his new bronze headstone. How was his middle names usually spelled?
2. Identify the first name of his mother and father.
3. Name the city and state where Elvis was born.
4. What was the exact date of Elvis's birth?
5. Name the church Elvis attended as a child.
6. What is the first name of Elvis's ex-wife?
7. Give the first name of their daughter.
8. What was the inscription on a stone near the original grave site of Elvis's mother?
9. How old was Elvis at the time of his death?
10. Indicate the exact date of Elvis's death.

2. THE EARLY ELVIS EXPLOSION

1. Name the recording service where Elvis cut that first record for his mother's birthday.
2. What were the titles of both sides of the first record Elvis cut there?
3. Give the name of the recording service's office manager who "discovered" Elvis.
4. Name the record company also owned by a man connected with the recording service.
5. Identify this record company owner, who was to play a big part in Elvis's early career.
6. Name the original two members of Elvis's backup group and the instruments they played. What is the name of the drummer who soon joined the group?
7. Elvis and this group were known as the Blue ———— Boys. Before that, Elvis was sometimes billed as The ———— Cat.
8. Name the Memphis disc jockey who became Elvis's manager and the call letters of the station where he worked.
9. What is the name of the country music show on which Elvis appeared under contract as a regular? From what city did the show originate?
10. Elvis made his first commercial stage appearance in Memphis at the ————Park Shell. Name Elvis's first hit record, released in August, 1954.

3. KINFOLK

1. Give the first and middle name of Elvis's twin brother who was still born.
2. Name Elvis's twin cousins who sing and play the guitar.
3. What was the maiden name of Elvis's mother?
4. What is the middle name of Elvis's father?
5. Name Elvis's two cousins who were part of his personal staff.
6. Give the first name and middle name of Elvis's parental grandmother.
7. What was the first name of Elvis's parental grandfather?
8. Give the titles of both sides of the record cut by Elvis's grandfather.
9. Name the label that released his grandfather's record.
10. The younger sister of Elvis's mother married the brother of Elvis's father. Name the couple.

4. LOVE MATCH

Fill in the blank by matching it to the list of words, completing the title of the love song Elvis sang.

1. "I'll _____ Love"
2. "_____ Love"
3. "I Love You _____"
4. "Love Me _____"
5. "Have I Told You _____ That I Love You?"
6. "I Need Your Love _____"
7. "A Big _____ O' Love"
8. "_____ of Your Love"
9. "_____ Love, Big Heartache"
10. "I Love Only _____ Girl"

a. Big
b. Tonight
c. Thrill
d. Hunk
e. Burning
f. One
g. Lately
h. Take
i. Tender
j. Because

5. THE NAME GAME — WOMEN

Fill in the blank with the name of the woman Elvis sang about in the song title.

1. "Long, Tall ————"
2. "———— in the Morning"
3. "Sweet ————" (Give names from two songs both be-
   "Sweet ————"   ginning with "Sweet.")
4. "———— and Johnny"
5. "————, the Gardener's Daughter"
6. "I'll Take You Home Again, ————"
7. "Santa ————"
8. "————, Cindy"
9. "Polk Salad ————"
10. "Proud ————"

6. LEADING MAN MATCH-UP

Match the film to the name of the leading man Elvis portrayed.

1. *Harum Scarum*   a. Johnny
2. *The Trouble with Girls*   b. Dr. John Carpenter
3. *Wild in the Country*   c. Johnny Tyronne
4. *It Happened at the World's Fair*   d. Mike Windgren
5. *Girls! Girls! Girls!*   e. Mike Edwards
6. *Kid Galahad*   f. Mike McCoy
7. *Change of Habit*   g. Ross Carpenter
8. *Spinout*   h. Glenn Tyler
9. *Frankie and Johnny*   i. Walter Hale
10. *Fun in Acapulco*   j. Walter Gulick

7. COLONEL PARKER

1. Give Colonel Parker's first and middle name.
2. What state bestowed the rank of honorary colonel on Parker in 1953?
3. What was the name of the traveling show owned by the Colonel's uncle?
4. Name the two leading country and western singers Colonel Parker represented before Elvis.
5. What is Colonel Parker's official job title?
6. How much money did Colonel Parker sell Elvis's contract to RCA for?
7. What is the name of Colonel Parker's wife?
8. With what legendary showman is Colonel Parker often compared?
9. In what capacity did Colonel Parker receive a screen credit on each Presley film?
10. Name Colonel Parker's two cats.

8. GOING PLACES

Fill in the blank naming the location mentioned in Elvis's song title.

1. "O Little Town of ———"
2. "——— Rain"
3. "Viva ——— ———"
4. "———, Tennessee"
5. "Never Been to ———"
6. "——— Special"
7. "You Can't Say No in ———"
8. "Fort ——— Chamber of Commerce"
9. "New ———"
10. "Heart of ———"

9. GIRLFRIENDS! GIRLFRIENDS! GIRLFRIENDS!

Match the movie to the actress who played Elvis's love interest.

1. *Jailhouse Rock*
2. *G.I. Blues*
3. *It Happened at the World's Fair*
4. *Fun in Acapulco*
5. *Viva Las Vegas*
6. *Tickle Me*
7. *Easy Come, Easy Go*
8. *Double Trouble*
9. *Speedway*
10. *The Trouble with Girls*

a. Nancy Sinatra
b. Jocelyn Lane
c. Ann-Margret
d. Judy Tyler
e. Marlyn Mason
f. Annette Day
g. Ursula Andress
h. Joan O'Brien
i. Dodie Marshall
j. Juliet Prowse

10. HIGH SCHOOL DAYS

1. Name the high school Elvis attended.
2. In what city is the school located?
3. On what street is the school situated?
4. Give the year Elvis was graduated from high school.
5. What was name of Elvis's date for the high school senior prom?
6. Name the housing project where Elvis lived during the majority of the time he attended high school.
7. As a high school student, Elvis wore the sides of his hair slicked back into a ——— tail.
8. What was the name of the high school football team for which Elvis briefly played?
9. Name the year, make, and model of the car Elvis drove in high school.
10. Give the initials identifying the cadet corps program Elvis was a member of in high school.

11. BABY TALK

Fill in the blank to complete the title of Elvis's song for big babies.

1. "———, Baby"
2. "——— a Baby"
3. "Ain't That ——— You, Baby"
4. "I've Got to ——— My Baby"
5. "It's Your Baby, You ——— It"
6. "I've Got ——— About You, Baby"
7. "My Baby ——— Me"
8. "Baby, Let's Play ———"
9. "Rock-a- ——— Baby"
10. "Bosa ——— Baby"

12. CINEMA SONGS

Name the Elvis movie in which the following songs appeared:
1. "Slowly But Surely"
2. "Banana"
3. "I Think I'm Gonna Like It Here"
4. "I'll Take Love"
5. "Chesay"
6. "Rubberneckin' "
7. "We're Coming in Loaded"
8. "Let Yourself Go"
9. "Stop Where You Are"
10. "Happy Ending"

13. PRESLEY'S PASSION

Elvis's friendship with the following young women attracted a lot of attention. Match each name to the correct description.

1. Venetia Stevenson
2. Margrit Buergin
3. Yvonne Lime
4. Diane Goodman
5. Dotty Harmony
6. Nancy Sharp
7. Barbara Hearn
8. Judy Spreckles
9. Vera Tchechowa
10. Sheila Ryan

a. Appeared in *Loving You*
b. Later married James Caan
c. German starlet
d. Socialite
e. From Memphis
f. German teen-ager
g. Former wife of Russ Tamblyn
h. Las Vegas showgirl
i. Miss Georgia
j. Wardrobe assistant

14. THE NAME GAME — MEN

Fill in the blank with the name of the man Elvis sang about in the song's title.

1. "Just Tell Her ——— Said Hello"
2. "——— Fit the Battle"
3. "I, ———"
4. "Stay Away, ———"
5. "——— Boy"
6. "Bosom of ———"
7. "Good Time ———'s Got the Blues"
8. "——— and Evil"
9. "Ready ———"
10. "——— B. Goode"

15. ELVIS IN THE ARMY

1. Give Elvis's official army induction date.
2. Name the barber who gave Elvis his first regulation army haircut.
3. Where was Elvis shipped to boot camp?
4. Where did Elvis receive basic combat training?
5. Name the album based on Elvis's press conference at the Brooklyn Army Terminal, September 22, 1958.
6. What was the name of the U.S. troop ship on which Elvis sailed to Germany?
7. Name Elvis's army buddy who later became his road manager.
8. Name Elvis's army buddy who later became his guitarist.
9. Elvis entered the army as a private. Name the highest rank he rose to during his two years of military service.
10. What was the official date of Elvis's discharge from the army?

16. PRISCILLA

1. Give Priscilla's maiden name.
2. What is Priscilla's middle name?
3. How old was Priscilla when she first met Elvis?
4. In what country did Priscilla and Elvis initially meet?
5. What rank did Priscilla's father hold in the air force at the time Priscilla first met Elvis?
6. Name the high school Priscilla attended in Memphis.
7. What year did Priscilla graduate from high school?
8. Name the school where Priscilla studied modeling and dance.
9. Name the karate instructor with whom Priscilla has been romantically linked.
10. What is the name of the Beverly Hills boutique Priscilla opened with a partner?

17. ANATOMY LESSON

Fill in the blank naming the part of the anatomy mentioned in the title of Elvis's song.
1. "Scratch My ————"
2. "Loving ————"
3. "I Washed My ———— in the Muddy Water"
4. "Up Above My ————"
5. "Wear My Ring Around Your ————"
6. "Spanish ————"
7. "The First Time Ever I Saw Your ————"
8. "His ———— in Mine"
9. "I Got a Feeling in My ————"
10. "In Your ————"

18. ELVIS ON TELEVISION

1. Name the television show Elvis was turned down for after auditioning.
2. Elvis made his first TV appearance in January, 1956, on the *Tommy and Jimmy Dorsey* ——— *Show*.
3. Name the comedian sometimes known as "Uncle Miltie" on whose television show Elvis appeared.
4. What was the name of the character Elvis played in a sketch on Steve Allen's TV show?
5. Give the name of the television show hosted by Ed Sullivan on which Elvis performed.
6. Fill in the blanks with the name of the television publication in the title of this RCA promotional release to radio stations cherished by collectors: "——— ——— Presents Elvis Presley."
7. What famed singer welcomed Elvis home from the army with a television special in which they appeared together?
8. Elvis wore a black ——— suit on his 1968 TV special.
9. How was Elvis's history-making concert broadcast around the world?
10. What was the name of Elvis's 1973 TV special?

19. THOSE WONDERFUL YEARS

Match the Elvis film to the year of its release.

1. *Blue Hawaii*	a.	1956
2. *Paradise, Hawaiian Style*	b.	1957
3. *It Happened at the World's Fair*	c.	1960
4. *Double Trouble*	d.	1961
5. *Love Me Tender*	e.	1962
6. *Elvis: That's the Way It Is*	f.	1963
7. *Jailhouse Rock*	g.	1964
8. *Follow That Dream*	h.	1966
9. *Flaming Star*	i.	1967
10. *Viva Las Vegas*	j.	1970

20. TRIPLE TREATS

Fill in the blank completing one third of the thought in Elvis's triple-treat song title.

1. "Shake, Rattle and ———"
2. "———! Girls! Girls!"
3. "I slipped, I stumbled, I ———"
4. "Vino, ——— y Amor"
5. "———, Look and Listen"
6. "Flip, ——— and Fly"
7. "I Want You, I Need You, I ——— You"
8. "Steadfast, Loyal and ———"
9. "Hey, ———, Hey"
10. "Turtles, Berries and ———"

21. TITLE TUNES

Does the film feature a title tune? Answer true or false after the name of each Elvis movie.
1. *Live a Little, Love a Little*
2. *Tickle Me*
3. *The Trouble with Girls*
4. *Change of Habit*
5. *Charro*
6. *Harum Scarum*
7. *Speedway*
8. *Kid Galahad*
9. *Spinout*
10. *It Happened at the World's Fair*

22. THE LITERARY ELVIS

Match the names of the books about Elvis to their authors
1. *My Life with Elvis*   a. James W. Bowser (editor)
2. *Elvis—The Films and
      Career of Elvis Presley*   b. James R. Parish
3. *Starring Elvis*   c. Kathleen Bauman
4. *The Private Elvis*   d. Red and Sonny West,
      (Originally published as,   Dave Hebler, as told to
      Elvis and the Colonel)   Steve Dunleavy
5. *The Illustrated Elvis*   e. Becky Yancey
6. *Elvis: What Happened?*   f. Paul Lichter
7. *Elvis—A Biography*   g. Steven and Boris
                                     Zmijewsky
8. *Elvis in Hollywood*   h. W. A. Harbinson
9. *On Stage with Elvis Presley* i. May Mann
10. *The Elvis Presley Scrapbook* j. Jerry Hopkins

23. COUNT THE FUN

Fill in the blank with the correct numerical answer to complete Elvis's song title.
1. "——— Trouble"
2. "——— Sleepy Heads"
3. "I Was Born Almost ——— Thousand Years Ago"
4. "——— -Sided Love Affair"
5. "One Boy, ——— Little Girls"
6. "The ——— Noel"
7. "For the ——— and Last Time"
8. "——— Is Enough"
9. "Don't Think ———, It's All Right"
10. "An American ———"

24. ELVIS'S EYEFULS

Name the movie each actress appeared in with Elvis.
1. Hope Lange
2. Carolyn Jones
3. Quentin Dean
4. Ina Balin
5. Barbara Eden
6. Lizabeth Scott
7. Marianna Hill
8. Debra Paget
9. Fran Jeffries
10. Barbara Stanwyck

25. MEMORIES OF ELVIS

Match the following entertainers and others to their special link in keeping the memory of Elvis alive.

 1. Larry Seth   a. Factors Etc., Inc.—Presley Merchandiser
 2. Rick Saucedo   b. Elvis Wade
 3. Johnny Rusk   c. "Heartbreak Hotel"/Heart Association
 4. Wade Cummins d. Tribute at Tropicana
 5. Eric Parks   e. "Elvis Alive"
 6. Lee Geissler   f. *Elvis The Legend Lives*
 7. Gregg Peters   g. England's "Elvis"
 8. Tommy Durden h. Presley sculpture for Memphis
 9. P. J. Proby   i. Seattle-based look-alike act
10. Alan Meyer   j. "The Big El"

26. PET PROJECT

Fill in the blank with the name of the pets, beasts, or other wildlife mentioned in Elvis's song title.
1. "(Let Me Be Your) Teddy ———"
2. "——— Man"
3. "Milk ——— Blues Boogie"
4. "Hound ———"
5. "Show ———"
6. "A ——— Life"
7. "Too Much ——— Business"
8. "——— Call"
9. "The——— fighter Was a Lady"
10. "——— Instinct"

27. SONGS ABOUT ELVIS

Match the songs about Elvis to their recording artists and composers.

1. "From Graceland to the Promised Land"
2. "I Saw Elvis Presley Last Night"
3. "The Tupelo Mississippi Flash"
4. "I Want Elvis Presley for Christmas"
5. "My Boy, Elvis"
6. "The King Is Gone"
7. "The King Is Coming Back"
8. "My Baby's Crazy 'Bout Elvis"
9. "The E. P. Express"
10. "Elvis Presley for President"

a. Ronnie McDowell
b. Billy Boyle
c. The Holly Twins
d. Billy and Eddie
e. Gary Lewis and The Playboys
f. Lou Monte
g. Carl Perkins
h. Merle Haggard
i. Jerry Reed
j. Janis Martin

28. MARRIAGE AND DIVORCE

1. Name the Las Vegas hotel where Elvis and Priscilla got married.
2. What was the exact date of their marriage?
3. Name the hotel owner in whose private suite the wedding took place.
4. What was the name of the Nevada Supreme Court justice who performed the wedding ceremony?
5. Give the first name of Priscilla's sister who served as her maid of honor.
6. Name the two members of Elvis's entourage who jointly served as his best men.
7. Was it a double-ring ceremony?
8. Give the ages of Elvis and Priscilla at the time of their marriage.
9. What was the address of the couple's new home in the Trousdale Estates section of Southern California?
10. Name the exact date the divorce of Elvis and Priscilla became final.

29. DON'T . . .

Do fill in the blank with the missing word from the song Elvis sang with "Don't" in its title.

1. "I Don't Care if the Sun ——— Shine"
2. "Don't Be ———"
3. "Don't ——— Me Now"
4. "———, I Don't Care"
5. "I Don't ——— Be Tied"
6. "Please Don't Drag That ——— Around"
7. "If You Think I Don't ——— You"
8. "Please Don't Stop ——— Me"
9. "You Don't Know ———"
10. "I Really Don't Want to ———"

30. CASTING CALL

Each of these actors and actresses appeared in two movies apiece with Elvis. The exception is Shelly Fabares, who appeared in three. Here are the performers. Now name their Presley films.
1. Shelley Fabares
2. Steve Brodie
3. Dolores Hart
4. L. Q. Jones
5. Joan Blackman
6. Bill Bixby
7. Yvonne Craig
8. Will Hutchins
9. Mary Ann Mobley
10. Gary Lockwood

31. LISA

1. What is the middle name of Elvis's daughter?
2. How long after Elvis's marriage to Priscilla was Lisa born?
3. Give the year Lisa was born.
4. What was the month and exact day of Lisa's birth?
5. Name the Memphis hospital where Priscilla gave birth to Lisa.
6. Give the exact time of Lisa's birth.
7. What was Lisa's exact weight at birth?
8. Providing all other conditions are met, what is the earliest age Lisa may come into control of Elvis's estate?
9. Name the actor friend of Elvis's who died the day after Priscilla and baby Lisa returned home from the hospital.
10. Did Elvis and Priscilla have any other children together?

32. COLOR BLIND

Fill in the blank with the name of the missing color from the title of the song Elvis sang.

1. "———— Bells"
2. "Long ———— Limousine"
3. "A Little Bit of ————"
4. "———— Hawaii"
5. "Milky ———— Way"
6. "When My Blue Moon Turns to ———— Again"
7. "———— Rose of Texas"
8. "———— Eyes Crying in the Rain"
9. "Green ———— Grass of Home"
10. "———— Moon of Kentucky"

33. DEE

1. What is Dee's real first name?
2. In what country did Dee meet Elvis's father?
3. Was Dee a divorcée or a widow when she married Vernon?
4. Give the exact date of Dee's secret marriage to Vernon.
5. Name the city and state where the marriage took place.
6. Did Elvis attend the wedding?
7. Name the Florida resort area where Dee and Vernon spent their honeymoon.
8. Give the first names as well as the last name of Dee's three sons from her first marriage.
9. Did Dee have any children with Vernon?
10. Did Elvis officially adopt his stepbrothers?
11. Identify the year in which Vernon's divorce from Dee became final. In what country was the divorce obtained?

34. STARS AND STRIPES

Match the officers to the Elvis films in which they appear.
1. Sergeant Benson
2. Sergeant McGraw
3. Lieutenant Moretti
4. Captain Heret
5. Major Kincaid
6. Lieutenant Rivera
7. Captain Roach
8. Sergeant Bailey
9. Captain Jack
10. Lieutenant Tracy Richards

a. *Spinout*
b. *Kissin' Cousins*
c. *Charro*
d. *Girl Happy*
e. *Easy Come, Easy Go*
f. *Change of Habit*
g. *Love Me Tender*
h. *G. I. Blues*
i. *Double Trouble*
j. *Harum Scarum*

35. MUSIC & SONG

Fill in the blank with the name of the musical instrument or reference to the special tune Elvis sang about in the title.
1. "Shake That ———"
2. "——— Song of the Year"
3. "Hawaiian ——— Song"
4. "A ——— Tune"
5. "——— of the Islands"
6. "Help Me, Mr. Song ———"
7. "——— Man"
8. "There Ain't Nothing Like a ———"
9. "Singing ———"
10. "My Desert ———"

36. REEL MOTHERS AND FATHERS

Name the movie in which each of the following stars plays one of Elvis's parents. Arthur O'Connell appears in two films cast as Elvis's father. The others appear in one movie apiece.

1. Angela Lansbury
2. Arthur O'Connell
3. Mildred Dunnock
4. John McIntyre
5. Katy Jurado (stepmother)
6. Roland Winters
7. Glenda Farrell
8. Burgess Meredith
9. Dolores Del Rio
10. Dean Jagger

37. WHO'S DIRECTING?

Match these Elvis movies to their directors.

1. *King Creole*
2. *G.I. Blues*
3. *Flaming Star*
4. *Roustabout*
5. *Kid Galahad*
6. *Fun in Acapulco*
7. *Viva Las Vegas*
8. *Girl Happy*
9. *Frankie and Johnny*
10. *The Trouble with Girls*

a. John Rich
b. Fred de Cordova
c. Norman Taurog
d. Phil Karlson
e. Boris Sagal
f. Peter Tewksbury
g. Michael Curtiz
h. Richard Thorpe
i. Don Siegel
j. George Sidney

38. ROLE CALL

Match the actress to the name of the character she portrayed in a movie with Elvis.

1. Mary Ann Mobley
2. Mary Tyler Moore
3. Donna Douglas
4. Deborah Walley
5. Yvonne Craig
6. Diane McBain
7. Millie Perkins
8. Shelley Fabares
9. Joan Blackman
10. Dolores Hart

a. Les
b. Valerie
c. Diane St. Clair
d. Princess Shalimar
e. Nellie
f. Frankie
g. Rose Grogan
h. Sister Michelle
i. Betty Lee
j. Azalea Tatum

39. THE REEL ELVIS

Name the movie in which Elvis portrayed the following character.
1. Rusty Wells
2. Joe Lightcloud
3. Lucky Jordan
4. Jesse Wade
5. Steve Grayson
6. Lonnie Beale
7. Charlie Rogers
8. Danny Fisher
9. Vince Everett
10. Pacer Burton

40. MOVIE MUSIC MATCH-UP

Match the song to the Elvis movie in which it is featured.
1. "I'm Not the Marrying Kind"   a. *Clambake*
2. "Ito Eats"   b. *Loving You*
3. "Didya Ever?"   c. *Double Trouble*
4. "Hard Knocks"   d. *Jailhouse Rock*
5. "(Let Me Be Your) Teddy Bear"   e. *Kid Galahad*
6. "A Little Less Conversation"   f. *G.I. Blues*
7. "Riding the Rainbow"   g. *Blue Hawaii*
8. "Confidence"   h. *Roustabout*
9. "One More Day"   i. *Follow That Dream*
10. "It Won't Be Long"   j. *Live a Little, Love a Little*

41. FRIENDS & RELATIONS

Fill in the blank with the name of a friend or specific relative Elvis sang about in the song title.
1. "Kissin' ———"
2. "——— Liked the Roses"
3. "My Little ———"
4. "In My ———'s House"
5. "He's Your ———, Not Your Dad"
6. "Don't Cry, ———"
7. "Little ———"
8. "That's All Right (———)"
9. "My ———"
10. "The ——— of My Best Friend"

42. FILM CALENDAR

Arrange the following Elvis films in the proper chronological order according to the year of their release.
1. *G. I. Blues*
2. *Frankie and Johnny*
3. *Harum Scarum*
4. *The Trouble with Girls*
5. *Speedway*
6. *Kid Galahad*
7. *King Creole*
8. *Kissin' Cousins*
9. *Loving You*
10. *Easy Come, Easy Go*

43. SOLID GOLD HITS

Provide the missing word in the titles of these Elvis recordings that sold more than one million copies apiece.
1. "Treat Me ———"
2. "All ——— Up"
3. "——— Rock"
4. "I Got ———"
5. "I ——— of You"
6. "It's Now or ———"
7. "——— Luck Charm"
8. "Return to ———"
9. "I ——— Know"
10. "Playing for ———"

44. ORIENTAL ODYSSEY

Match these talented performers to the names of the characters they played in Elvis's films.

1. James Shigeta
2. Beulah Quo
3. Benson Fong
4. Vicky Tiu
5. Lani Kai
6. Irene Tsu
7. Kam Tong
8. Linda Wong
9. Philip Ahn
10. Ginny Tiu

a. Walter Ling
b. Moki
c. Carl Tanimi
d. Mai Ling
e. Madame Yung
f. Lehua
g. Danny Kohana
h. Sue-Lin
i. Kin Yung
j. Pua

45. HEART TO HEART

Fill in the blank with the missing word, completing the song
title Elvis sang from the heart.
1. "———— Heart"
2. "Your ———— Heart"
3. "Cross My Heart and Hope to ————"
4. "You're a Heart ————"
5. "One ———— Heart for Sale"
6. "Heartbreak ————"
7. "I'll ———— You in My Heart"
8. "That's When Your Heartaches ————"
9. "Home Is ———— the Heart Is"
10. "One ———— Heart"

46. ROLL THOSE CREDITS

Match the following Presley movies to their respective studios. Some studios are responsible for more than one Elvis film here.

1. *Tickle Me*
2. *Girl Happy*
3. *Girls! Girls! Girls!*
4. *Love Me Tender*
5. *Charro*
6. *Change of Habit*
7. *Clambake*
8. *Roustabout*
9. *Spinout*
10. *Wild in the Country*

a. NBC-Universal
b. Paramount
c. 20th Century-Fox
d. United Artists
e. Metro-Goldwyn Mayer
f. National General
g. Allied Artists

47. LUCK OF THE IRISH

Mc who? Fill in the rest of the last names of the two Mc characters Elvis portrayed. And complete the last names beginning with Mc of the actors and actresses who appeared with Elvis in the movies indicated on the left.

1. Elvis in *G.I. Blues*   Tulsa Mc_____
2. Elvis in *Spinout*   Mike Mc_____
3. *Change of Habit*   Barbara Mc_____
4. *Blue Hawaii*   Howard Mc_____
5. *Girls! Girls! Girls!*   Ann Mc_____
6. *Flaming Star*   John Mc_____
7. *Spinout*   Diane Mc_____
8. *Charro*   J. Edward Mc_____
9. *Change of Habit*   Ruth Mc_____
10. *Easy Come, Easy Go*   Frank Mc_____

48. ELVIS ON LOCATION

Match each film to its main locale according to the story line.

1. *Harum Scarum*
2. *Elvis: That's the Way It Is*
3. *Charro*
4. *It Happened at the World's Fair*
5. *Love Me Tender*
6. *King Creole*
7. *Stay Away, Joe*
8. *Clambake*

9. *G.I. Blues*
10. *Girl Happy*

a. Texas
b. Miami
c. New Orleans
d. Middle East
e. Fort Lauderdale
f. West Germany
g. Seattle
h. International Hotel, Las Vegas
i. Arizona
j. Mexico

49. GINGER ALDEN

1. Give the exact date Elvis had planned to announce his engagement to Ginger according to her account.
2. The engagement announcement was to have been made at Elvis's scheduled concert in what city?
3. How many carats is Ginger's diamond ring from Elvis?
4. According to Ginger's family, Elvis had planned to wed Ginger on what day?
5. Give the first names of Ginger's two sisters.
6. What beauty contest title did one of Ginger's sisters formerly hold?
7. Name the month and year Ginger first met Elvis.
8. Name the make and model of the car Elvis gifted Ginger with.
9. In which state did Elvis vacation with Ginger and her family in March, 1977?
10. What real-life role did Ginger's father play in Elvis's army career?

50. NICKNAMES AND NUMBERS

1. A clergyman proclaimed Elvis; The Whirling ———— of Sex.
2. How tall was Elvis?
3. His gyrations on stage led to the nickname Elvis the ————.
4. Give Elvis's exact army serial number.
5. What did critics call Elvis's staff of bodyguards?
6. What degree and color belt did Elvis hold in karate?
7. What number highway is close to Elvis's Memphis estate?
8. Give the exact house number of Elvis's Memphis estate.
9. What did Elvis and his buddies call themselves when riding motorcycles?
10. In the early days, critics called Elvis's sound: Grunt and ———— Music.
11. Not counting the two documentaries, how many films did Elvis make?

51. THE JORDANAIRES

A. Name the early Jordanaires.

Did the Jordanaires provide vocal backgrounds for the following Elvis movies? Answer true or false after each film title.
1. *Tickle Me*
2. *Spinout*
3. *Speedway*
4. *Girl Happy*
5. *G. I. Blues*
6. *Jailhouse Rock*
7. *Live a Little, Love a Little*
8. *Stay Away, Joe*
9. *Loving You*
10. *Easy Come, Easy Go*

52. ELVISMS

1. Name the American movie star romantically linked with Elvis—who never appeared in any of his films.
2. What is the name of the Memphis rink where Elvis went roller skating with his buddies?
3. Elvis was known throughout the world as the ——— of Rock and Roll.
4. Name the former presidential yacht Elvis purchased and turned over to Danny Thomas for St. Jude Hospital.
5. Which noted evangelist did Elvis once pray with in Las Vegas?
6. Name the chain of sewing centers through which the album, "Elvis Singing Flaming Star and Others" was released in 1968.
7. According to a lyric Elvis sang in "Polk Salad Annie," what does polk salad look something like?
8. Elvis enjoyed peanut butter and ——— sandwiches.
9. Barbra Streisand wanted Elvis to star with her in a remake of what film classic?
10. Name the singer/actor who got the movie role Barbra Streisand had originally slated for Elvis.

53. ELVIS ON THE JOB

Name the movie from the career Elvis pursues in it.
1. Photographer
2. Doctor
3. Singer on a showboat
4. Movie star
5. Tourist guide
6. Air Force officer
7. Navy frogman
8. Charter boat pilot
9. Helicopter charter pilot
10. Water-ski instructor

54. PRODUCERS ON PARADE

Match these Elvis films to their producers.

1. *Love Me Tender*   a. Pandro Berman
2. *Loving You*   b. Sam Katzman
3. *Jailhouse Rock*   c. Joe Connelly
4. *Wild in the Country*   d. Judd Bernard and Irwin Winkler
5. *Kissin' Cousins*   e. Hal Wallis
6. *Tickle Me*   f. Douglas Laurence
7. *Spinout*   g. Ben Schwalb
8. *Double Trouble*   h. David Weisbart
9. *Stay Away, Joe*   i. Joe Pasternak
10. *Change of Habit*   j. Jerry Wald

55. WHAT . . .

1. . . . street is Heartbreak Hotel located on?
2. . . . is the name of Elvis's Memphis estate?
3. . . . was the name of Elvis's pet chimpanzee?
4. . . . sport did Elvis play on his own court at home in Memphis?
5. . . . is the name of Elvis's private four-engine jet?
6. . . . was the name of Elvis's ranch?
7. . . . street is Elvis's Memphis estate located?
8. . . . was the movie *Love Me Tender* to have been called originally?
9. . . . colorful souvenirs did Elvis often throw out to his fans from the stage during concerts?
10. . . . was the name of the hound dog Elvis sang "Hound Dog" to on the *Steve Allen Show*?

56. MOOD FOOD

Fill in the blank to complete the food item or flavor in Elvis's song title.
1. "Three ——— Patches"
2. "Tutti ———"
3. "Do the ———"
4. "——— Hill"
5. "Cotton ——— Land"
6. "Song of the ———"
7. "Queenie Wahine's ———"
8. "Craw ———"
9. "——— bake"
10. "Hot ———"

57. THE PRESLEY PAPERS

1. How much did Elvis's first guitar cost?
2. What was the name of the firm Elvis worked for as a truck driver after graduating from high school?
3. As a publicity stunt, Colonel Parker once formed The Elvis Presley ———— Fan Club.
4. Filming in shifts, how many sets of twins were used to portray the one infant in *G.I. Blues*?
5. Which Elvis album does not have his name on the front or back cover?
6. Elvis's most famous suit was made of gold ————.
7. What division did Elvis serve with in the army?
8. Name the actress who covered Elvis's army homecoming press conference for a radio network.
9. Give the official cause of Elvis's death.
10. Name the Memphis cemetery where Elvis was originally laid to rest—before being buried on the grounds of his Memphis estate.

58. FILLED WITH LOVE

Fill in the blank with the missing word of love, completing the title of the song Elvis sang.
1. "Lover ———"
2. "——— of Love"
3. "What ——— My Love"
4. "——— Fall in Love"
5. "True Love Travels on a ——— Road"
6. "You Don't Have to ——— You Love Me"
7. "Could I ——— in Love"
8. "It's ——— Love"
9. "The Girl I ——— Loved"
10. "Your Love's Been a Long Time ———"

PRESLEY PHOTO QUIZ

1. Elvis and Ann-Margret sizzled in *Viva Las Vegas*. Off-screen, what did Elvis send Ann-Margret for luck before each new opening of her nightclub act?

[ANSWERS FOR PHOTO QUIZ
APPEAR ON PAGE *154*]

2. Name the second documentary film made about Elvis in which this scene appears.

3. Who is the girl in Elvis's crystal ball? What movie did they appear in together?

4. Identify the film named after the prizefighter Elvis portrays.

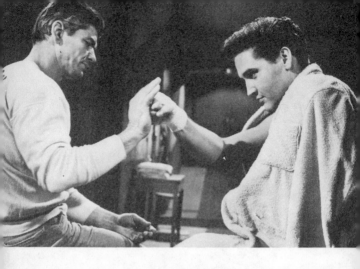

5. Cut through the red tape: Name the actor who tapes Elvis's hand in preparation for his next big fight.

6. In *Harum Scarum* Elvis soars to new heights of fame. Identify the three dancing girls he meets who have jewel-like names.

7. Who is the blonde sharing Elvis's passionate embrace?
Name the film in which she plays a bad influence on his
life.

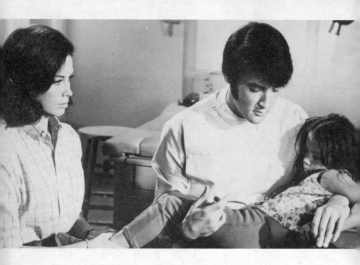

8. We're not pulling your leg: Who is the actress attending to Lorena Kirk as Elvis cradles the child in his arms? In which movie is this scene featured?

9. What attraction did Elvis tour with this little girl as indicated in the title of the film?

10. Elvis makes a daring deep-sea dive off a cliff in which film?

11. Name the movie whose title is based on Elvis's job with a carnival. Here he gives the high sign to his girlfriend in the film. Who is the actress?

12. Elvis is no puppet when it comes to love in *G.I. Blues*. Name the actress who portrays the loving doll he plans to marry after the army show is over.

59. IDENTITY CRISIS

1. Identify Elvis's sun sign.
2. Elvis bought many of his clothes at Lansky Brothers, located on what Memphis street popular with blues musicians?
3. Name the character Elvis's former bodyguard Red West plays on "Black Sheep Squadron?"
4. Elvis's private security force wore pins featuring a lightning bolt along with the letters TCB. What did the letters and bolt mean?
5. David Weisbart, who produced several of Elvis's movies, was also the producer of which legendary James Dean film?
6. Name the Tennessee town in which Elvis's national fan club is headquartered.
7. Identify the man who produced Elvis's records since 1962.
8. Who is Elvis's private jet named after?
9. Identify the rock and roll group that had a hit record of "Little Egypt" before Elvis sang the song in *Roustabout*.
10. Elvis recorded "It's Now or Never" which is based on what classical Italian song?

60. NIGHT & DAY

Fill in the blank completing the title of the song Elvis sang about day or night.
1. "Night ———"
2. "——— Night"
3. "Night ———"
4. "——— Night"
5. "Any Day ———"
6. "——— of Night"
7. "Twenty Days and ——— Nights"
8. "There's a Brand New Day on the ———"
9. "——— Night"
10. "It's ——— Night"

61. LINDA THOMPSON

1. What is Linda's middle name?
2. What state did Linda represent in the Miss U.S.A. beauty pageant?
3. Indicate Linda's ranking in the finals for the Miss U.S.A. title.
4. Linda was Elvis's companion for how many years?
5. What is the name of the black rag doll Elvis bought Linda in Las Vegas?
6. Give the alternate spelling of Linda Thompson's first name in some published reports.
7. Name the theater where Linda first met Elvis at one of his private screenings.
8. What did Elvis and Linda name their dog?
9. Give Linda's favorite nickname for Elvis.
10. In what city did Elvis buy a house for Linda?

62. WALK AWAY

Fill in the blank with the missing word in the titles of Elvis's walk-away hits.
1. "Blue ———— Shoes"
2. "High Heel————"
3. "Big ————"
4. "If You Walk in My ————"
5. "———— on My Heels"
6. "Girl Next ———— Went a-Walking"
7. "I'm Gonna Walk ———— Golden Stairs"
8. "You'll Never Walk ————"
9. "———— Ballad"
10. "If the Lord Wasn't Walking by My ————"

63. MERRY CHRISTMAS

Fill in the blank to complete the Christmas message Elvis sang in the title.

1. "——— Christmas"

   (Name the two colors of Christmas.)

   "——— Christmas"
2. "I'll Be ——— for Christmas"
3. "On a ——— Christmas Night"
4. "Merry Christmas, ———"
5. "Holly ——— and Christmas Trees"
6. "The Wonderful ——— of Christmas"
7. "It Won't ——— Like Christmas"
8. "If ——— Day Was Like Christmas"
9. "If I Get Home on Christmas ———"
10. "Here Comes ——— Claus"

64. MEN & WOMEN, BOYS & GIRLS

Fill in the blank with the missing word concerning the men, women, boys and girls Elvis sang about in the song title.

1. "What Every Woman ——— For"
2. "Big ——— Man"
3. "——— Little Girl"
4. "Mean Woman ———"
5. "Smokey ——— Boy"
6. "Long——— Girl (with the short dress on)"
7. "Go ———, Young Man"
8. "Hard ——— Woman"
9. "The ——— Girl in Town"
10. "A Boy Like ———, A Girl Like You."

65. LONELINESS & TEARS

Fill in the blanks to complete these lonely and tearful song titles Elvis sang.

1. "Crying in the ———"
2. "Summer Kisses, ——— Tears"
3. "I'm Gonna ——— Right Down and Cry Over You"
4. "Just ——— Me Lonesome"
5. "I'm So Lonesome, I Could ———"
6. "Finders ———, Losers Weepers"
7. "Lonesome ———"
8. "Blue Eyes Crying in the ———"
9. "Lonely ———"
10. "The ——— of Your Cry"

66. NAME . . .

1. . . . the location of Elvis's ranch.
2. . . . the type of football Elvis played.
3. . . . the organization which voted Elvis one of the Ten Outstanding Young Men of America in 1970.
4. . . . the Memphis amusement park Elvis rented for his daughter.
5. . . . Elvis's favorite amusement-park ride.
6. . . . the black female singing group that appeared with Elvis in Las Vegas and on tour.
7. . . . male gospel quartet long associated with Elvis's shows.
8. . . . the leader of this gospel quartet.
9. . . . Elvis's personal physician in Memphis.
10. . . . the city and state in which Elvis Presley Park is located.

67. TODAY, TONIGHT, & TOMORROW

Fill in the blank with the missing word that's right for these Elvis songs of today, tomorrow, and tonight.
1. "Are You ——— Tonight?"
2. "Tomorrow is a ——— Time"
3. "Good ——— Tonight"
4. "I ——— Her Today"
5. "Tomorrow and ———"
6. "I ——— Your Love Tonight"
7. "Tomorrow ——— Comes"
8. "I'm ——— in Love Tonight"
9. "——— Today"
10. "Tonight Is So Right for ———"

68. HEAVEN ABOVE

Fill in the blanks, completing the titles of these heavenly songs Elvis sang.

1. "Take My Hand, ——— Lord"
2. "Jesus Knows What I ———"
3. "Where Could I ——— But to the Lord"
4. "Believe in the Man in the ———"
5. "When the Saints Go ——— In"
6. "Reach ——— to Jesus"
7. "There Is No God But ———"
8. "Why ——— Lord?"
9. "This Is ——— Heaven"
10. "Where Did ——— Go, Lord?"

69. LOVE ME TENDER

1. How many brothers does Elvis have in the film?
2. What is the brothers' last name?
3. Name the brother whose girlfriend marries Elvis.
4. Name the actress married to Elvis.
5. What is the name of the character Elvis portrays?
6. Who plays the youngest brother?
7. Name the Confederate cavalry regiment in which Elvis's brothers served.
8. What do Elvis's brothers rob?
9. Where does Cathy hide the money?
10. Name the location where the brothers plan to meet.

70. LOVING YOU

1. What does Elvis come to deliver at the rally?
2. What job did Elvis hold before joining the band?
3. Name the character Elvis plays.
4. What is Glenda's last name?
5. In what capacity is Glenda employed?
6. Name the guitarist portrayed by Paul Smith.
7. What color is the bright sports shirt Elvis wears?
8. Name the color (and color upholstery) of the convertible Elvis is gifted with.
9. Name the actress who plays Susan Jessup, the band's singer.
10. In real life, what did this actress leave show business to become?

71. JAILHOUSE ROCK

1. Name Elvis's cell mate.
2. What is the name of the character Elvis plays?
3. Name the club where Elvis applies for a job after getting out of jail.
4. Who owned the club?
5. Name the actor who portrays the disc jockey.
6. Name the singing star Peggy represents.
7. What label does this singer record for?
8. Where does Peggy's father teach?
9. To which label is Elvis's first record sold?
10. Name the label for which Elvis records his second record.

72. KING CREOLE

1. What is the name of the character Elvis portrays?
2. The movie is based on what well-known novel?
3. Who authored the novel?
4. Name the nightclub where Elvis first works.
5. What is his job at the club?
6. In what city is the club located?
7. Name the young hoodlum played by Vic Morrow.
8. Identify the actor who portrays Elvis's father.
9. Give the name of the club where Elvis is offered a singing job.
10. Who plays Ronnie? Name the popular TV series in which this actress starred.

73. G.I. BLUES

1. Elvis is based in West ———.
2. Name the character Elvis portrays.
3. Give the names of Elvis's two army buddies.
4. Where is a G. I. suddenly transferred?
5. Name the actress who plays Lili, the cabaret dancer.
6. In real life, what superstar was she briefly engaged to?
7. How much money will Elvis and his buddies stand to win on the wager they make?
8. What does Elvis have to do to win?
9. Name the actress whose infant Elvis baby-sits for.
10. Is the baby a girl or boy?

74. FLAMING STAR

1. Elvis is —————— percent Indian.
2. Name the Indian tribe involved in the massacre.
3. Name the state in which the story takes place.
4. What is the first name of the character Elvis portrays?
5. Name the actress who plays Elvis's mother.
6. Give the last name of Elvis's family.
7. How does Elvis send his wounded brother Clint into town?
8. Name the actress who is helpful to Clint.
9. What popular television series did this actress star in?
10. What does the flaming star symbolize to Elvis?

75. WILD IN THE COUNTRY

1. What does Uncle Rolfe sell to a widow as a cure for cancer?
2. Name the dance hall where Elvis takes Betty Lee.
3. What is the name of the actress who portrayed Betty Lee and the title of the film she starred in based on a diary?
4. Elvis shows talent in which creative field?
5. Name the character Elvis plays.
6. What is Irene Sperry's job title? Who was the actress in the role?
7. Give the name of the TV series this actress starred in.
8. Name the adopted daughter of Joan Crawford who portrays Monica George.
9. Name the former Olympic athlete who portrays Davis.
10. Judge Parker was played by the real-life former father-in-law of Lauren Bacall. Name him.

76. BLUE HAWAII

1. What does Maile lose?
2. Name the Chinese houseboy.
3. What is the name of the company owned by Elvis's father?
4. Name the character Elvis portrays.
5. What job does Elvis get after coming out of the service?
6. What does Elvis give Maile's grandmother for her birthday?
7. Name the country in which Elvis bought the gift.
8. Identify the hotel where Elvis meets Abigail Prentice.
9. Name the actress who plays the girl Elvis plans to marry.
10. What does Elvis intend to call his new business?

77. FOLLOW THAT DREAM

1. Name the county in Arkansas where Elvis is from.
2. Give the last name of Elvis's family.
3. Name the twins.
4. What is the medical reason for Elvis being on total disability?
5. Name the judge.
6. What is the first name of the character Elvis plays?
7. What job title does Alicia Claypoole hold?
8. Give the name of the actress who portrays Alicia.
9. Name the famous young star who is the real-life daughter of this actress.
10. Name the two gangsters.

78. KID GALAHAD

1. Name the hotel where Kid Galahad trains.
2. What does the sign at the training camp proclaim?
3. Name the community where the training camp is located.
4. By what name is Elvis known before he becomes Kid Galahad?
5. Name the cook.
6. How old is Elvis when his parents die?
7. Where is Elvis brought up by his aunt?
8. Name the Mexican fighter.
9. What is the name of the actress who plays Dolly Fletcher?
10. Elvis's "cut man" has his ———— broken by gangsters.

79. GIRLS! GIRLS! GIRLS!

1. What is the first name of the actress who portrays a character with the same first name?
2. Give the last name of this actress.
3. Now give the last name of the girl she plays.
4. Give her exact street address and apartment number in the film.
5. Name the fleabag hotel where she pretends to live when first meeting Elvis.
6. Name the restaurant where Elvis meets her for lunch.
7. What is the name of the character Elvis portrays?
8. Name the sailboat Elvis and his father built.
9. Where are the Starvoses moving because of her ill heath?
10. Name the boat Elvis skippers for charters.

80. IT HAPPENED AT THE WORLD'S FAIR

1. Name the group supplying vocal backgrounds for the film in addition to the Jordanaires.
2. Where does this world's fair take place?
3. Who plays the little Chinese girl Elvis takes on a tour of the fair?
4. What does this child's father do for a living?
5. Name the character Elvis portrays.
6. Elvis is a ——— pilot.
7. What is the name of the actor in the role of Elvis's co-pilot?
8. How does this co-pilot keep getting into trouble?
9. Name the actress who plays Dorothy Johnson and is pursued by Elvis.
10. Actress Joan O'Brien wears a uniform signifying she is a ———.

81. FUN IN ACAPULCO

1. Elvis suffers from a fear of ————.
2. Name the job Elvis formerly held as a circus performer.
3. Who is cast in the role of the bullfighter?
4. Name the song Elvis sings inspired by this bullfighter.
5. What is the name of the character Elvis portrays?
6. Who plays the young shoeshine boy?
7. How many feet does Alejandro Rey plunge off the cliff?
8. Identify the one-named lifeguard he enacts.
9. What position does Ursula Andress hold at the hotel?
10. Where does Elvis want to take Ursula?

82. KISSIN' COUSINS

1. Give the first name of the hillbilly Elvis portrays.
2. What is the last name of the hillbilly family?
3. Give the full name of the military officer also played by Elvis.
4. In what branch of the military does Elvis serve?
5. According to one of the song titles from the film, what is in the mountains?
6. What activity is the hillbilly family engaged in that they wish to keep from the government?
7. What does the government want to use the mountain for?
8. What color wig does Elvis wear as the hillbilly cousin?
9. Give the abbreviation of the branch of military service in which Cynthia Pepper is cast.
10. Yvonne Craig's first name in the picture is also the name of a flowering shrub. Identify it.

83. VIVA LAS VEGAS

1. What is the name of the stripper?
2. Name the club where this stripper works.
3. How much more money does Elvis need for a new rac-ing-car motor?
4. What is the name of the race Elvis plans to enter?
5. Name the character Elvis portrays.
6. What is Ann-Margret's job at the hotel?
7. Identify the title of the duet Elvis sings with Ann-Mar-gret.
8. Give the first name of Elvis's mechanic.
9. What is the surprise gift left for Ann-Margret from El-vis?
10. Identify the number starting position Elvis's car is assigned in the race.

84. ROUSTABOUT

1. Name the espresso café where Elvis performs.
2. What is the name of the satirical song Elvis sings that angers students?
3. Elvis plays Charlie Rogers. What last name has he also used?
4. Name the actress who portrays the carnival owner. What TV series did this actress star in with Lee Majors?
5. What's a "mitt camp?"
6. Define "grab joint".
7. Sue Ann Langdon is cast in the role of a palm reader named Madame ———.
8. Name the girl in the shower who later went on to become known as a sex symbol in a number of films.
9. What is the name of the rival carnival?
10. Who plays Little Egypt?

85. GIRL HAPPY

1. Name the former child star who plays Sergeant Benson.
2. What dance does Elvis sing about?
3. What is Sunny Daze covered with while doing a strip-tease?
4. On what charge is Shelley Fabares arrested?
5. Name the character Elvis portrays.
6. In what city does Shelley Fabares's father own a night-club?
7. Where does Elvis dig an escape tunnel?
8. Name the famed singer whose son appears in the film.
9. What is the son's first name?
10. Geography lesson: ———— are mistakenly pictured in Fort Lauderdale, Florida.

86. TICKLE ME

1. Name the actress who plays the owner of the ranch and health spa.
2. Is the spa coed?
3. What job is Elvis hired for at the ranch?
4. Name the character Elvis portrays.
5. What is the name of the ghost town?
6. What does Jocelyn Lane expect to find in the ghost town?
7. From which deceased relative does she have a letter?
8. According to a song title from the movie, how long do I feel I've known you?
9. What is the name of the crooked sheriff?
10. What is the feeling mentioned in a song title from the movie?

87. HARUM SCARUM

1. Name the Lord of the Assassins.
2. What organization is Zacha a member of in good standing?
3. Name the country Elvis is invited to visit as a guest of King Toranshad.
4. Name the movie star Elvis portrays.
5. What is the name of his latest film?
6. Mary Ann Mobley is cast in the role of Princess ————.
7. Name the actor (a midget) who played Baba and also had a role in *Roustabout*.
8. What is the name of the actor who portrays Prince Drana? Name his ex-wife and the Presley film in which she appeared.
9. "So Close, Yet So Far" from where, according to the movie song?
10. Name the Las Vegas Hotel where Elvis appears with the dancing girls.

88. FRANKIE AND JOHNNY

1. What musical instrument does Cully play?
2. What is Elvis's vice?
3. Name the character Elvis portrays.
4. Identify the dance group bearing the name of its director as listed in the screen credits.
5. Who plays the role of Frankie?
6. Name the popular TV series that the star who played Frankie appeared in.
7. The gypsy fortune teller predicts Elvis will change his luck after meeting a woman with what color hair?
8. Name the actress whose hair color matches the fortune teller's description.
9. Elvis's life is saved from the bullet by the lucky ——— he wears.
10. What theatrical mecca should "look out" according to the title of this song from the movie?

89. PARADISE, HAWAIIAN STYLE

1. What type of aircraft does Elvis fly?
2. Name the actor who plays Elvis's business partner.
3. Susanne Leigh is cast as Elvis's ————.
4. What is the name of the character Elvis portrays?
5. How many girls does Elvis have referring customers to his charter service?
6. Identify the actresses who play Elvis's glamorous business recruiters.
7. Name the government agency John Doucette works for.
8. Some critics accused this film of being a remake of what earlier Presley picture?
9. Complete the title of this song from the film: "House of ————."
10. Name the title of the bonus song on the movie soundtrack album.

90. SPINOUT

1. Name the actress who portrays a character with the same first name.
2. What musical instrument does Deborah Walley play?
3. Identify the name of the character enacted by Elvis.
4. Name the title of the book being researched by one of the women after Elvis.
5. Name the Bob Dylan tune that appears as a bonus song on the movie soundtrack album.
6. Dodie Marshall is cast in the role of Susan. Name the other Presley picture in which Dodie appears.
7. Will Hutchins plays Lieutenant Tracy Richards. Name the TV series in which Hutchins starred.
8. Name the famed comedienne whose younger sister was formerly married to Will Hutchins.
9. Shelley Fabares is spoiled by her father's ————.
10. What is the name of the actor who portrays Shelley's father? Identify the TV series in which this late actor also played Shelley's dad.

91. EASY COME, EASY GO

1. Name the song from this movie with the same title as a best selling novel by Jacqueline Susann.
2. What form of physical fitness is Dodie Marshall studying?
3. Identify the song from the film which mentions Dodie's exercise twice in its title.
4. Who portrays Madame Neherina?
5. What are the coins found to be made of?
6. The coins are worth less than $————.
7. Name the cargo on the ship in addition to the coins in the treasure chest.
8. What is the money used as a down payment for?
9. Name the character Elvis portrays.
10. What is the name of the actor who plays Elvis's business partner?

92. DOUBLE TROUBLE

1. In what city does Elvis first meet Annette Day?
2. Name the character Elvis portrays.
3. How many brothers make up the detective team?
4. Give the last name of these brothers who play the zany sleuths.
5. What crime do the brothers suspect Elvis of?
6. Name the city in Belgium where Annette Day is being sent off to school.
7. Elvis and Annette are reunited traveling by ———.
8. "Old MacDonald" from the film is an updated version of what popular song?
9. Name the actress who portrays the other woman interested in Elvis.
10. What is the name of the inspector?

93. CLAMBAKE

1. Name the character Elvis portrays.
2. Elvis's father made his millions in what business?
3. Name the actor Elvis swaps identities with.
4. In trading identities, what does Elvis now teach?
5. Name the actress who plays Elvis's first student.
6. What is the name of the race Elvis wins?
7. In real life, actor Jack Good produced what rock-music television series?
8. Add the appropriate roman numerial after the name of James Jamison, the character portrayed by Bill Bixby.
9. Name the popular space-age TV series in which Bill Bixby starred.
10. Bette Davis was once married to the actor cast in the role of Elvis's business partner. Name him.

94. STAY AWAY, JOE

1. What Indian tribe does Elvis belong to?
2. Name the character Elvis plays.
3. Elvis returns to the reservation after traveling the ————— circuit.
4. Name the congressman.
5. Elvis's father is portrayed by the Oscar nominee for best supporting actor in the movie *Rocky*. Name him.
6. Identify Elvis's former bodyguard turned writer who was cast in the role of Jackson He-Crow. What is the real first name of this former bodyguard?
7. Name the song from the movie with the same title as the hit recorded by The Singing Nun.
8. Name the actress who portrays the tavern owner. In real life, she was the wife of the late Mike Todd before Elizabeth Taylor.
9. What animal does Elvis barbecue?
10. A jail sentence is almost handed down to Elvis's family for selling what government property?

95. SPEEDWAY

1. Elvis races ———— cars.
2. Name the character Elvis portrays.
3. Who plays Elvis's manager?
4. This manager gambles Elvis's winnings on ———— races.
5. Name the famed singer whose daughter is cast as Elvis's love interest, Susan Jacks.
6. What is the first name of this singer's daughter?
7. What does Elvis owe the government money for?
8. How much money does Elvis owe?
9. Whom does Susan Jacks work as an undercover agent for?
10. Name the titles of the two duets Elvis sings with Susan.

96. LIVE A LITTLE, LOVE A LITTLE

1. Name the novel upon which this movie is based.
2. Identify the author of the novel whose former wife Nora Ephron married Carl Bernstein, one of the two "Washington Post" investigative reporters credited with breaking the Watergate scandal wide open.
3. What is the first name of the character Elvis portrays?
4. Who plays the publisher of the girlie magazine?
5. Name the old-time singer who is cast as the conservative publisher.
6. In stage appearances, this singer used a ———— instead of a microphone.
7. Name the relative of Elvis who had a brief nonspeaking role in the film.
8. Who plays the model in hot pursuit of Elvis?
9. In what creative capacity does Elvis work for the magazines?
10. "———— World" is one of the featured songs from the movie.

97. CHARRO

1. Name the border town to which Elvis rides.
2. Identify the saloon Elvis enters.
3. What is the name of the actor who portrays the gang leader?
4. Name the barber who practices medicine without a license.
5. Elvis is romantically linked with Tracey, who is played by what actress?
6. Name the character Elvis portrays.
7. What was the name given to the historic Mexican cannon?
8. The cannon had been used to fire the last shot against ——— to free Mexico.
9. Give the financial value of the cannon.
10. The cannon was stolen from ——— Palace.

98. THE TROUBLE WITH GIRLS

1. What is the subtitle of this movie?
2. Name the character played by Vincent Price.
3. A song in the film suggests that you "Clean Up Your Own ———"
4. Name the type of traveling tent show Elvis managed.
5. What is the name of the character Elvis portrays?
6. How does the illicit love affair end?
7. Give the last name of the mayor.
8. Maude is played by Joyce Van Patten. What is the first name of her real-life brother, a long-time TV star?
9. Who portrays Elvis's girlfriend, Charlene?
10. Mr. Drewcolt is played by what actor whose son David is a star in his own right.

99. CHANGE OF HABIT

1. Name the nun portrayed by Mary Tyler Moore.
2. What flop show did Mary Tyler Moore star in on Broadway?
3. Identify the actresses who played the other two nuns.
4. Give the initials indicating Elvis's profession.
5. What sort of facility does Elvis head?
6. Name the character Elvis plays.
7. Identify the type of musical mass Elvis leads.
8. Give the last name of the lieutenant played by Edward Asner.
9. In what TV series bearing the name of another *Change of Habit* star did Edward Asner appear?
10. Name the supermarket Sister Barbara pickets.

ANSWERS

QUIZ 1

1. Aaron; Aron
2. Gladys and Vernon
3. Tupelo, Mississippi
4. January 8, 1935
5. The First Assembly of God
6. Priscilla
7. Lisa
8. "She was the sunshine of our home."
9. 42
10. August 16, 1977

QUIZ 2

1. The Memphis Recording Service
2. "My Happiness" and "That's When Your Heartaches Be-gin"
3. Marion Keisker
4. Sun Records
5. Sam Phillips
6. Bill Black—bass; Scotty Moore—guitar; D. J. Fontana
7. Moon; Hillbilly
8. Bob Neal; WMPS
9. *Louisiana Hayride;* Shreveport
10. Overton
    "That's All Right (Mama)"

QUIZ 3

1. Jesse Garon
2. Jerry and Terry Presley
3. Smith
4. Elvis
5. Gene and Billy Smith
6. Minnie Mae
7. Jessie
8. "The Billy Goat Song" and "Swinging in the Orchard"
9. Legacy Records
10. Cletis and Vester

QUIZ 4

1. h
2. e
3. j
4. i
5. g
6. b
7. d
8. c
9. a
10. f

QUIZ 5

1. Sally
2. Mary
3. Caroline
   Angeline
4. Frankie
5. Petunia
6. Kathleen
7. Lucia
8. Cindy
9. Annie
10. Mary

QUIZ 6

1. c
2. i
3. h
4. e
5. g
6. j
7. b
8. f
9. a
10. d

QUIZ 7

1. Thomas Andrew
2. Tennessee
3. The Great Parker Pony Circus
4. Hank Snow and Eddy Arnold
5. Personal manager
6. $35,000
7. Marie
8. P. T. Barnum
9. Technical advisor
10. Midnight and Chrissie

QUIZ 8

1. Bethlehem
2. Kentucky
3. Las Vegas
4. Memphis
5. Spain
6. Frankfurt
7. Acapulco
8. Lauderdale
9. Orleans
10. Rome

QUIZ 9

1. d
2. j
3. h
4. g
5. c
6. b
7. i
8. f
9. a
10. e

QUIZ 10

1. L. C. Humes
2. Memphis
3. Manasas
4. 1953
5. Dixie Locke
6. Lauderdale Courts
7. Duck
8. The Humes Tigers
9. 1942 Lincoln coupe
10. ROTC

QUIZ 11

1. Reconsider
2. Like
3. Lovin'
4. Find
5. Rock
6. Thing
7. Left
8. House
9. Hula
10. Nova

QUIZ 12

1. *Tickle Me*
2. *King Creole*
3. *Fun in Acapulco*
4. *Easy Come, Easy Go*
5. *Frankie and Johnny*
6. *Change of Habit*
7. *Girls! Girls! Girls!*
8. *Speedway*
9. *Paradise, Hawaiian Style*
10. *It Happened at the World's Fair*

QUIZ 13

1. g
2. f
3. a
4. i
5. h
6. j
7. e
8. d
9. c
10. b

QUIZ 14

1. Jim
2. Joshua
3. John
4. Joe
5. Danny
6. Abraham
7. Charlie
8. Adam
9. Teddy
10. Johnny

QUIZ 15

1. March 24, 1958
2. James Peterson
3. Fort Chaffee, Arkansas
4. Fort Hood, Texas
5. "Elvis Sails"
6. *General Randall*
7. Joe Esposito
8. Charlie Hodge
9. Sergeant
10. March 5, 1960

QUIZ 16

1. Beaulieu
2. Ann
3. 14
4. Germany
5. Captain
6. Immaculate Conception High School
7. 1963
8. Patricia Stevens Finishing and Career School
9. Mike Stone
10. Bis and Beaus

QUIZ 17

1. Back
2. Arms
3. Hands
4. Head
5. Neck
6. Eyes
7. Face
8. Hand
9. Body
10. Arms

QUIZ 18

1. *Arthur Godfrey's Talent Scouts*
2. *Stage*
3. Milton Berle
4. Tumbleweed
5. *Toast of the Town*
6. *TV Guide*
7. Frank Sinatra
8. Leather
9. Via satellite
10. *Elvis: Aloha from Hawaii*

QUIZ 19

1. d
2. h
3. f
4. i
5. a
6. j
7. b
8. e
9. c
10. g

QUIZ 20

1. Roll
2. Girls
3. Fell
4. Dinero
5. Stop
6. Flop
7. Love
8. True
9. Hey
10. Gumbo

QUIZ 21

1. False
2. False
3. False
4. True
5. True
6. False
7. True
8. False
9. True
10. False

QUIZ 22

1. e
2. g
3. a
4. i
5. h
6. d
7. j
8. f
9. c
10. b

QUIZ 23

1. Double
2. Five
3. Ten
4. One
5. Two
6. First
7. Millionth
8. Once
9. Twice
10. Trilogy

QUIZ 24

1. *Wild in the Country*
2. *King Creole*
3. *Stay Away, Joe*
4. *Charro*
5. *Flaming Star*
6. *Loving You*
7. *Paradise, Hawaiian Style*
8. *Love Me Tender*
9. *Harum Scarum*
10. *Roustabout*

QUIZ 25

1. j
2. f
3. i
4. b
5. h
6. a
7. e
8. c
9. g
10. d

QUIZ 26

1. Bear
2. Tiger
3. cow
4. Dog
5. bird
6. Dog's
7. Monkey
8. Wolf
9. Bull
10. Animal

QUIZ 27

1. h
2. e
3. i
4. c
5. j
6. a
7. d
8. b
9. g
10. f

QUIZ 28

1. The Aladdin
2. May 1, 1967
3. Milton Prell
4. David Zenoff
5. Michelle
6. Joe Esposito and Marty Lacker
7. Yes
8. 32 and 21
9. 1174 Hillcrest Road
10. October 19, 1973

QUIZ 29

1. Don't
2. Cruel
3. Leave
4. Baby
5. Wanna
6. String
7. Need
8. Loving
9. Me
10. Know

QUIZ 30

1. *Girl Happy; Spinout; Clambake*
2. *Blue Hawaii; Roustabout*
3. *Loving You; King Creole*
4. *Flaming Star; Stay Away, Joe*
5. *Blue Hawaii; Kid Galahad*
6. *Clambake; Speedway*
7. *It Happened at the World's Fair; Kissin' Cousins*
8. *Spinout; Clambake*
9. *Girl Happy; Harum Scarum*
10. *Wild in the Country; It Happened at the World's Fair*

QUIZ 31

1. Marie
2. Exactly nine months
3. 1968
4. February 1
5. Baptist Memorial
6. 5:01 P.M.
7. 6 pounds, 15 ounces
8. 25
9. Nick Adams
10. No

QUIZ 32

1. Silver
2. Black
3. Green
4. Blue
5. White
6. Gold
7. Yellow
8. Blue
9. Green
10. Blue

QUIZ 33

1. Davada
2. Germany
3. Divorcée
4. July 3, 1960
5. Huntsville, Alabama
6. No
7. Panama City
8. Ricky, David, and Billy Stanley
9. No
10. No
11. 1977; Dominican Republic

QUIZ 34

1. d
2. h
3. f
4. j
5. g
6. c
7. i
8. b
9. e
10. a

1. Tambourine
2. Love
3. Wedding
4. Whistling
5. Drums
6. man
7. Guitar
8. Song
9. Tree
10 Serenade

1. *Blue Hawaii*
2. *Follow That Dream; Kissin' Cousins*
3. *Love Me Tender*
4. *Flaming Star*
5. *Stay Away, Joe*
6. *Blue Hawaii*
7. *Kissin' Cousins*
8. *Stay Away, Joe*
9. *Flaming Star*
10. *King Creole*

QUIZ 37

1. g
2. c
3. i
4. a
5. d
6. h
7. j
8. e
9. b
10. f

QUIZ 38

1. d
2. h
3. f
4. a
5. j
6. c
7. i
8. b
9. g
0. e

QUIZ 39

1. *Girl Happy*
2. *Stay Away, Joe*
3. *Viva Las Vegas*
4. *Charro*
5. *Speedway*
6. *Tickle Me*
7. *Roustabout*
8. *King Creole*
9. *Jailhouse Rock*
10. *Flaming Star*

QUIZ 40

1. i
2. g
3. f
4. h
5. b
6. j
7. e
8. a
9. d
10. c

QUIZ 41

1. Cousins
2. Mama
3. Friend
4. Father
5. Uncle
6. Daddy
7. Sister
8. Mama
9. Boy
10. Girl

QUIZ 42

1. *Loving You*
2. *King Creole*
3. *G. I. Blues*
4. *Kid Galahad*
5. *Kissin' Cousins*
6. *Harum Scarum*
7. *Frankie and Johnny*
8. *Easy Come, Easy Go*
9. *Speedway*
10. *The Trouble with Girls*

QUIZ 43

1. Nice
2. Shook
3. Jailhouse
4. Stung
5. Beg
6. Never
7. Good
8. Sender
9. Gotta
10. Keeps

QUIZ 44

1. g
2. e
3. i
4. h
5. c
6. j
7. a
8. f
9. b
10. d

QUIZ 45

1. Wooden
2. Cheatin'
3. Die
4. breaker
5. Broken
6. Hotel
7. Hold
8. Begin
9. Where
10. Track

QUIZ 46

1. g
2. e
3. b
4. c
5. f
6. a
7. d
8. b
9. e
10. c

QUIZ 47

1. Cauley
2. Coy
3. Nair
4. Near
5. Crea
6. Intyre
7. Bain
8. Kinley
9. Devitt
10. Hugh

QUIZ 48

1. d
2. h
3. j
4. g
5. a
6. c
7. i
8. b
9. f
10. e

QUIZ 49

1. August 27, 1977
2. Memphis
3. 11½
4. Christmas Day
5. Terry and Rosemary
6. Miss Tennessee
7. November, 1976
8. Lincoln Continental
9. Hawaii
0. He was the officer who inducted Elvis into the Army in 1958.

QUIZ 50

1. Dervish
2. Six feet
3. Pelvis
4. U. S. 53310761
5. The Memphis Mafia
6. Ninth-degree Black Belt
7. 51
8. 3764
9. El's Angels
0. Groin
1. 31

QUIZ 51

A. Hoyt Hawkins, Neal Matthews, Gordon Stoker and Hugh Jarrett
1. False
2. True
3. True
4. False
5. True
6. False
7. False
8. True
9. True
10. True

QUIZ 52

1. Natalie Wood
2. The Rainbow
3. King
4. *The Potomac*
5. Rev. Rex Humbard
6. Singer
7. A turnip green
8. Banana
9. *A Star Is Born*
10. Kris Kristofferson

QUIZ 53

1. *Live a Little, Love a Little*
2. *Change of Habit*
3. *Frankie and Johnny*
4. *Harum Scarum*
5. *Blue Hawaii*
6. *Kissin' Cousins*
7. *Easy Come, Easy Go*
8. *Girls! Girls! Girls!*
9. *Paradise, Hawaiian Style*
10. *Clambake*

QUIZ 54

1. h
2. e
3. a
4. j
5. b
6. g
7. i
8. d
9. f
10. c

QUIZ 55

1. Lonely
2. Graceland
3. Scatter
4. Racquetball
5. The *Lisa Marie*
6. The Circle G
7. Elvis Presley Boulevard
8. *The Reno Brothers*
9. Scarves
10. Sherlock

QUIZ 56

1. Corn
2. Frutti
3. Clam
4. Blueberry
5. Candy
6. Shrimp
7. Papaya
8. fish
9. Clam
10. Dog

QUIZ 57

1. $12.95
2. Crown Electric Company
3. Midget
4. Three sets
5. "On Stage"
6. Lamé
7. Third Armored Division
8. Tina Louise
9. Heart attack
10. Forest Hill

QUIZ 58

1. Doll
2. Echoes
3. Now
4. Fools
5. Gravel
6. Say
7. Fall
8. Only
9. Never
10. Coming

QUIZ 59

1. Capricorn
2. Beale Street
3. Sgt. Andy Micklin
4. Taking Care of Business—Quick
5. *Rebel Without a Cause*
6. Madison
7. Felton Jarvis
8. His daughter
9. The Coasters
10. "O Sole Mio"

QUIZ 60

1. Life
2. Silent
3. Rider
4. One
5. Now
6. City
7. Twenty
8. Horizon
9. Such
10. Mid

QUIZ 61

1. Diane
2. Tennessee
3. Third runner-up
4. Five
5. Patty Alice
6. Lynda
7. The Memphian
8. Get Low
9. "Bunting" (as in baby bunting)
10. Memphis

QUIZ 62

1. Suede
2. Sneakers
3. Boots
4. Shoes
5. Wheels
6. Door
7. Dem
8. Alone
9. Barefoot
10. Side

QUIZ 63

1. White
   Blue
2. Home
3. Snowy
4. Baby
5. Leaves
6. World
7. Seem
8. Every
9. Day
10. Santa

QUIZ 64

1. Lives
2. Boss
3. Hey
4. Blues
5. Mountain
6. Legged
7. East
8. Headed
9. Meanest
10. Me

QUIZ 65

1. Chapel
2. Winter
3. Sit
4. Call
5. Cry
6. Keepers
7. Cowboy
8. Rain
9. Man
10. Sound

QUIZ 66

1. Walls, Mississippi
2. Touch
3. the United States Jaycees
4. Libertyland
5. Bumper cars—sometimes known as Dodgems
6. The Sweet Inspirations
7. The Stamps Quartet
8. J. D. Sumner
9. Dr. George Nichopoulos
10. Tupelo, Mississippi

QUIZ 67

1. Lonesome
2. Long
3. Rockin'
4. Met
5. Forever
6. Need
7. Never
8. Falling
9. Starting
10. Love

QUIZ 68

1. Precious
2. Need
3. Go
4. Sky
5. Marching
6. Out
7. God
8. Me
9. My
10. They

QUIZ 69

1. Three
2. Reno
3. Vance
4. Debra Paget
5. Clint
6. Elvis
7. Randall's Raiders
8. A federal payroll
9. In her dress
10. Hanna's Mill

QUIZ 70

1. Beer
2. He was a truck driver
3. Deke Rivers
4. Markle
5. As a press agent
6. Skeeter
7. Green
8. White with red upholstery
9. Dolores Hart
10. A nun

QUIZ 71

1. Hunk Houghton
2. Vince Everett
3. The Florita
4. Sam Brewster
5. Dean Jones
6. Mickey Alba
7. Geneva Records
8. At Bertrand College
9. Royal Records
10. Laurel Records

QUIZ 72

1. Danny Fisher
2. *A Stone for Danny Fisher*
3. Harold Robbins
4. The Blue Shade
5. Busboy
6. New Orleans
7. Shark
8. Dean Jagger
9. The King Creole
10. Carolyn Jones; The Addams Family

QUIZ 73

1. Germany
2. Tulsa McCauley
3. Rick and Cooky
4. Alaska
5. Juliet Prowse
6. Frank Sinatra
7. $300
8. Spend the night with Lili
9. Sigrid Maier
10. Boy

QUIZ 74

1. 50
2. Kiowa
3. Texas
4. Pacer
5. Dolores Del Rio
6. Burton
7. Tied to a horse
8. Barbara Eden
9. *I Dream of Jeannie*
10. Death

QUIZ 75

1. Bottles of tobacco juice
2. High Tension Grove
3. Millie Perkins; *The Diary of Anne Frank*
4. Writing
5. Glenn Tyler
6. Psychiatric case worker; Hope Lange
7. *Peyton Place*
8. Christina Crawford
9. Rafer Johnson
10. Jason Robards, Sr.

QUIZ 76

1. The top of her bikini
2. Ping Pong
3. The Great Southern Hawaiian Fruit Company
4. Chad Gates
5. Tourist guide
6. A music box
7. Austria
8. Hawaiian Village Hotel
9. Joan Blackman
10. Gates of Hawaii

QUIZ 77

1. Cranberry County
2. Kwimper
3. Eddy and Teddy Bascomb
4. A bad back
5. Judge Waterman
6. Toby
7. State Welfare Superintendent
8. Joanna Moore
9. Tatum O'Neal
10. Carmine and Nick

QUIZ 78

1. Grogan's Gaelic Gardens
2. The Cradle of Champions Since 1917
3. Cream Valley
4. Walter Gulick
5. Maynard
6. 14 months
7. Lowbridge, Kentucky
8. Sugarboy Romero
9. Lola Albright
10. Fingers

QUIZ 79

1. Laurel
2. Goodwin
3. Dodge
4. 136 Bay Street, Apartment 3
5. The New Plaza
6. The Grotto
7. Ross Carpenter
8. *The West Wind*
9. Arizona
10. *Kingfisher*

QUIZ 80

1. The Mello Men
2. Seattle
3. Vicky Tiu
4. He is a farmer
5. Mike Edwards
6. Bush
7. Gary Lockwood
8. By Gambling
9. Yvonne Craig
10. Nurse

QUIZ 81

1. Heights
2. Trapeze artist
3. Elsa Cardenas
4. "The Bullfighter Was a Lady"
5. Mike Windgren
6. Larry Domasin
7. 136
8. Moreno
9. Social director
10. To Florida

QUIZ 82

1. Jodie
2. Tatum
3. Josh Morgan
4. Air force
5. Gold
6. Moonshining
7. A missile base
8. Blond
9. WAC
10. Azalea

QUIZ 83

1. Miss Susie LeBang
2. The Silver Slipper
3. $3,800
4. The Las Vegas Grand Prix
5. Lucky Jordan
6. Pool manager
7. "The Lady Loves Me"
8. Shorty
9. A tree
10. Eleven

QUIZ 84

1. Mother's Tea House
2. "Poison Ivy League"
3. Main
4. Barbara Stanwyck; *Big Valley*
5. Palmistry tent
6. Hot dog stand
7. Mijanou
8. Raquel Welch
9. Carver's Combined Shows
10. Wilda Taylor

QUIZ 85

1. Jackie Coogan
2. The Clam
3. Newspapers
4. Disorderly conduct
5. Rusty Wells
6. Chicago
7. Under the jail
8. Bing Crosby
9. Gary
10. Mountains

QUIZ 86

1. Julie Adams
2. No
3. Handyman
4. Lonnie Beale
5. Silverado
6. Gold
7. Her grandfather
8. Forever
9. Deputy Sturdivant
10. Dirty

QUIZ 87

1. Sinan
2. Honorable Guild of Marketplace Thieves
3. Lunarkand
4. Johnny Tyronne
5. *Burning Sands*
6. Shalimar
7. Billy Barty
8. Michael Ansara; Barbara Eden, *Flaming Star*
9. Paradise
10. The Galaxy

QUIZ 88

1. Piano
2. Gambling
3. Johnny
4. Earl Barton Dancers
5. Donna Douglas
6. *The Beverly Hillbillies*
7. Red
8. Nancy Kovack
9. Charm
10. Broadway

QUIZ 89

1. Helicopter
2. James Shigeta
3. Secretary
4. Rick Richards
5. Three
6. Julie Parrish, Linda Wong, and Marianna Hill
7. The Federal Aviation Agency
8. *Blue Hawaii*
9. Sand
10. "Sand Castles"

QUIZ 90

1. Diane McBain
2. Drums
3. Mike McCoy
4. *The Perfect American Male*
5. "Tomorrow Is a Long Time"
6. *Easy Come, Easy Go*
7. *Sugarfoot*
8. Carol Burnett
9. Money
10. Carl Betz; The Donna Reed Show

QUIZ 91

1. "The Love Machine"
2. Yoga
3. "Yoga Is As Yoga Does"
4. Elsa Lanchester
5. Copper
6. 4,000
7. Coffee
8. An art center
9. Ted Jackson
10. Pat Harrington

QUIZ 92

1. London
2. Guy Lambert
3. Three
4. Wiere
5. Jewel smuggling
6. Brussels
7. Boat
8. "Old MacDonald Had a Farm"
9. Yvonne Romain
10. DeGrotte

QUIZ 93

1. Scott Heywood
2. Oil
3. Will Hutchins
4. Water-skiing
5. Shelley Fabares
6. The Orange Bowl Regatta
7. *Shindig*
8. III
9. *My Favorite Martian*
10. Gary Merrill

QUIZ 94

1. Navajo
2. Joe Lightcloud
3. Rodeo
4. Morissey
5. Burgess Meredith
6. "Sonny" West; Delbert
7. "Dominique"
8. Joan Blondell
9. A bull
10. Cattle

QUIZ 95

1. Stock
2. Steve Grayson
3. Bill Bixby
4. Horse
5. Frank Sinatra
6. Nancy
7. Income tax
8. $150,000
9. The Internal Revenue Service
10. "There Ain't Nothing Like a Song" and "Your Groovy Self"

QUIZ 96

1. *Kiss My Firm And Pliant Lips*
2. Dan Greenburg
3. Greg
4. Don Porter
5. Rudy Vallee
6. Megaphone
7. His father, Vernon
8. Michele Carey
9. As a photographer
10. Wonderful

QUIZ 97

1. Rio Seco
2. The Town House
3. Victor French
4. Opie Keetch
5. Ina Balin
6. Jesse Wade
7. The Victory Gun
8. Maximilian
9. $100,000
10. Chapultepec

QUIZ 98

1. (*And How to Get into It*)
2. Mr. Morality
3. Backyard
4. Chautauqua
5. Walter Hale
6. In Murder
7. Gilchrist
8. Dick
9. Marlyn Mason
10. John Carradine

QUIZ 99

1. Sister Michelle
2. *Breakfast at Tiffany's*
3. Barbara McNair and Jane Elliot
4. M. D.
5. A medical clinic
6. Dr. John Carpenter
7. Rock and Roll
8. Moretti
9. *The Mary Tyler Moore Show*
10. Ajax

PRESLEY PHOTO QUIZ

1. A floral display in the shape of a guitar
2. *Elvis on Tour*
3. Nancy Sinatra; *Speedway*
4. *Kid Galahad*
5. Charles Bronson
6. Emerald, Sapphire, and Amethyst
7. Tuesday Weld; *Wild in the Country*
8. Mary Tyler Moore; *Change of Habit*
9. The World's Fair (*It Happened at the World's Fair*)
10. *Fun in Acapulco*
11. *Roustabout*; Joan Freeman
12. Juliet Prowse

SIGNET Books You'll Want to Read

☐ **SINATRA: An Unauthorized Biography by Earl Wilson.**
Sinatra the swinger . . . the singer . . . the legend . . .
the man. The nationally syndicated columnist and best-
selling author reveals all in this sensational biography.
With eight pages of candid photos. (#E7487—$2.25)

☐ **BOUND FOR GLORY by Woody Guthrie, with a Foreword
by Pete Seeger.** The hard-driving, truth-telling autobiog-
raphy of America's great folk hero. It vividly brings to life
both his vibrant personality and a vision of America we
cannot afford to let die. Now a triumphant film from
United Artists starring David Carradine.
(#J7119—$1.95)

☐ **BOB DYLAN: An Intimate Biography by Anthony Sca-
duto.** The full story of Bob Dylan, the most influential
and elusive culture hero of our time. "I like your book.
That's the weird thing about it."—Bob Dylan
(#W5353—$1.50)

☐ **THE FILMGOER'S BOOK OF QUOTES by Leslie Halliwell.**
A dazzling collection of 700 quips, quotes, and quizzes
—by and about your favorite stars, past and present! A
Nostalgia Book Club Selection. (#E6702—$1.75)

☐ **TV MOVIES by Leonard Maltin.** Revised edition. Here is
your complete guide to everything you want to know
about more than 10,000 movies now being shown on
TV—the old and the new, the memorable and the not
so memorable. (#E6150—$2.25)

☐ **MOVIE COMEDY TEAMS by Leonard Maltin.** The inside
stories of the unforgettable comedians who made millions laugh! Lavishly illustrated, with filmography and
index. (#E6480—$1.75)

SIGNET Books of Special Interest to Film Fans

☐ **JACK NICHOLSON: The Search for a Superstar by Norman Dickens.** The fascinating truth about the man behind the killer smile! Here is the story of the man who became a new breed of Hollywood star. Frank and incisive, this book is unique in getting behind the smile and the super-cool front of this extraordinary actor to show the forces that drive him and the ambitions that continue to shape the most exciting acting career in films today. With 16 pages of photos!
(#W6726—$1.50)

☐ **SIDNEY POITIER: THE LONG JOURNEY by Carolyn H. Ewers.** The revealing, true story of his climb to the top. A hungry rebel, led by chance to the stage, by luck into films, by guts to the top . . . the personal story of one of America's finest actors and now director, Academy Award-winning Sidney Poitier.
(#Q6495—95¢)

☐ **KATE: The Life of Katharine Hepburn by Charles Higham.** Here is a vivid portrait of the most elegant, independent, and tempestuous superstar of them all—her life, her career, and the deeply moving story of her twenty-five-year love affair with Spencer Tracy. "Rich with her wit and excitement . . . and a deeply moving love story."—*Los Angeles Times*
(#J6944—$1.95)

☐ **JAMES DEAN: A Short Life by Venable Herndon.** The truth behind the whispered secrets of his private life, his rebellious public image and his sensational film career. With eight pages of rare personal photos and stills of his great starring roles.
(#W6518—$1.50)

THE NEW AMERICAN LIBRARY, INC.,
P.O. Box 999, Bergenfield, New Jersey 07621

Please send me the books I have checked above. I am enclosing $_____ (check or money order—no currency or C.O.D.'s). Prices and numbers are subject to change without notice. Please include the list price plus the following amounts for postage and handling: 35¢ for Signets, Signet Classics, and Mentors; 50¢ for Plumes, Meridians, and Abrams.

Name_____

Address_____

City_____ State_____ Zip Code_____
Allow at least 4 weeks for delivery